Two Hundred Houses

Rachel Sills

NEWTON-LE-WILLOWS

Published in the United Kingdom in 2015
by The Knives Forks And Spoons Press,
122 Birley Street,
Newton-le-Willows,
Merseyside,
WA12 9UN.

ISBN 978-1-909443-69-3

Copyright © Rachel Sills, 2015.

The right of Rachel Sills to be identified as the author of this work has been asserted by her in accordance with the Copyrights, Designs and Patents Act of 1988. All rights reserved. No part of this publication may be reproduced, stored in a retrieval system, transmitted in any form or by any means, electronic, photocopying, recording or otherwise, without prior permission of the publisher.

The cover image is by Dylan Harris. Please visit his website at http://dylanharris.org/ to see more of his excellent work.

for Poppy, Teddy and Flora

Two Hundred Houses

1. Mary's house has a feature staircase

2. Joan's house has guest towels in the bathroom

3. Marjorie's house is decorated in good taste, but there was once a toad in the cellar

4. Debbie's house is actually a flat

5. David's house is next to a school, which affects his broadband connection

6. Brendon's house was tiny, but had a very long garden

7. Jackie's house has floor-to-ceiling windows and finding curtains has been a problem

8. Monika's house was in Chorlton, but now she lives in Bristol

9. Charlie's house had a garden where a weeping willow took most of the light

10. Olive's house had a front parlour that was never used; there were Nuttall's Mintoes in a glass dish on the sideboard

11. Ailsa's house had a den and a blue lagoon pool

12. Andrea's house had cherry-print curtains in the bedroom, on which Oll once wiped his mouth

13. Souad's house had a Victorian-style street lamp in the front garden

14. Helen's house is a bungalow with an upstairs, but that's Helen all over

15. Kemi's house is on a corner, and her other house is also on a corner

16. Jason's house was opposite a flat belonging to an uninhibited woman

17. Gillian's house has a kitchen extension

18. Leona's house is pleasant and ordinary, but that's Leona all over

19. Linda's house is full of elephants

Two Hundred Houses

20. Marion junior's house has a transparent bathroom door

21. Marion senior's house had: a) a tea towel of the Mona Lisa; b) holy water fonts on the walls

22. Liz's house was a 1970s tribute to Laura Ashley

23. Claire's house has grapes growing in the conservatory

24. Rachel's house has bare plaster walls and a red velvet sofa

25. Kara's house has plasma TVs in quite a lot of the rooms

26. Carmelina's house was one of the first to have laminate flooring

27. Jo's house is a short walk from the sea

28. Deirdre's house is next door to a pub, but she doesn't seem to get much noise

29. Anna's house is immaculate

30. Oksana's house has a grand piano in the front room

31. Annabel's house is double fronted

32. Oriana's house has encaustic tiles in the downstairs loo

33. Sarah's house is built from Lancashire stone that glows gold in the sun; Bruce lives on a cushion in the front room

34. Cecilia's house had a Zen-style pebble garden at the front

35. Poppy's house has a man cave in the cellar and woodchip on the walls

36. Connie's house had a picture window overlooking the sand dunes

37. Tracey's house was on Condor Grove

38. Michelle's house was also on Condor Grove

39. Dougie's house was at the end of a cul-de-sac, in more ways than one

Two Hundred Houses

40. Brian's house had a dark blue kitchen

41. Johannes' house was a bargain, as he bought it from his landlord

42. Bianka's house was in the shadow of Old Trafford

43. Mary's house has a bike in the hall and smells of patchouli

44. Roman's house is near PC World

45. Siobhain's house is open to all-comers, and centres round the big square kitchen

46. Chervonne's house is a mystery

47. Karey's house has vintage hats on the picture rails

48. Elaine's house has parquet floors and a Buddha on the back lawn

49. Fokkina's house has a sun lounge and period features

50. Jeanette's house is full of children

51. Hannah's house has a garden with an ancient apple tree spreading across the lawn

52. Oliver's house was once the Moonie headquarters of Manchester

53. Karen's house has all the pictures very high up on the walls

54. Sandra's house had Victorian dolls standing round the perimeter of the back bedroom

55. Nicola's house has a mezzanine floor and a view of the meadow

56. Steve's house had a darts board in the garage

57. Michael's house has a garden that backs onto the national cycle path, which is handy

58. Jason's house had all the glass panels boarded up with cardboard

59. Dennis's house had a room built over the garage to house a snooker table

60. Rosemary's house is on an exclusive street – her neighbours employ chiropractors for their horses

61. Gabrielle's house is on the market

62. Mark's house is on an estate

63. Lee's house is a tribute to his mother's love of florals

64. Pat's house has a cellar converted into a party venue

65. Robert's house is a vicarage, and he is the vicar

66. Geoffrey's house was once a dental surgery; false teeth were found in the garden during renovations

67. Michelle's house had a bar in the back room, with optics and beer on tap

68. Nicky's house had a carport for his Ford Capri

69. Heather's house has a self-contained flat in the attic

Rachel Sills

70. Matthew's house is on a hill, although his room looks over the back

71. Norah's house had antique furniture and smelled of beeswax

72. John's house has a balcony overlooking the river and gets the sun for most of the day

73. Steve's house had a kitchen with terracotta tiles and cupboards with barley twist features

74. Steven's house is modern, and not really to his taste

75. Fenella's house is on the most desirable street in Didsbury

76. Sybil's house has the original 1930s bathroom

77. Frank's house was adjacent to a fish and chip shop

78. Nikki's house was on the street with the brothel

79. Susan's house is in Yorkshire, and has a green range in the kitchen

Two Hundred Houses

80. Beth's house had white vinyl sofas and smelled of Alsatian

81. Joel's house had frosted windows in the front room

82. Helene's house has a pink front door

83. Charley's house had a dead bee suspended in a chunk of amber on the front room mantelpiece

84. Simon's house was dominated by dark wood

85. Ron's house had an onyx telephone and matching ashtrays

86. Tara's house had Swiss cheese painted on the landing walls

87. Susan's house is opposite the cricket club, and when she was a child her house was round the corner from another cricket club

88. Heidi's house had macramé everywhere

89. Kevin's house is an executive home on The Close

Rachel Sills

90. Lenny's house had a machete in the cellar

91. Jan's house is under the flight path, which might affect its re-sale value

92. Elspeth's house was next to a wood

93. May's house had an old-fashioned bell and an "undefined" front garden

94. Bethany's house was a red-brick terrace on a slope

95. Shahrokh's house had a huge Persian rug in the lounge

96. Jason's house is full of shiny surfaces

97. Angie's house had a spiral staircase on the first floor, which was the thing in the 1970s

98. Justin's house had a tree house in the garden

99. Rita's house had a glass front door with a sunburst pattern

Two Hundred Houses

100. Nelly's house was number four,
     green door

101. Dan's house had room for a piano
     in the hall

102. Betty's house had beaded curtains
     and gentleman callers

103. George's house had a wooden
     deck and smelled of pine forests

104. Tony's house was a Georgian
     terrace and overlooked St Bride's

105. Linda's house had mood lighting
     and a kneel-in chair

106. Samara's house was once divided
     into flats, so the kitchen is upstairs

107. Helena's house is a Victorian villa
     in Cheshire

108. Naomi's house has patterned
     carpets and wallpaper throughout

109. Tommy's house was next to the
     Mormon Temple

110. Ruth's house has a studio in the
     attic with a sprung floor

111. Kim's house has off-road parking, although her car was still vandalised

112. Georgie's house had scripture on the wall

113. Milton's house has mahogany floors and a framed picture of Marilyn Monroe

114. Farhat's house had a chalkboard door in the kitchen

115. George's house had a hairdressing salon and a German Shepherd in the front room

116. Tina's house had plush carpets and neutral soft furnishings

117. Len's house is a narrowboat

118. Louise's house is decorated in Scandinavian style

119. Angela's house was a bed & breakfast in South Shore

Two Hundred Houses

120. Doc's house was out of bounds

121. Julie's house had an undetonated
hand grenade on the hearth

122. Gabrielle's house had an allotment
in the garden

123. Katherine's house was very dark

124. Ann's house had a pram in the
hall, in which there was a baby
with a sunken fontanelle

125. Sylvia's house has geraniums on
the kitchen windowsill

126. Simmy's house has Roman blinds
and two Chihuahuas in the front
window

127. Nina's house is in Brazil, but her
grandma lives in Chalfont St. Giles

128. Celia's house is near the grammar
school

129. Steve's house is authentic art
deco, inside and out

130. Winnie's house had fittings stolen
from Noel Coward

Rachel Sills

131. Sam's house has an extremely narrow stairwell

132. Andy's house is in a conservation area, which is making renovations tricky

133. Aoife's house has room in the driveway to park a campervan

134. Maureen's house had an annex from where she ran a small anti-aging business

135. Hilary's house had a cockatiel in a cage that could say hello

136. Helen's house has beer stacked in the downstairs loo

137. Linzi's house is full of skulls

138. Nan's house was compact, but perfect for her needs

139. Kathryn's house has Spanish-style tiles on the roof

Two Hundred Houses

140. Dolores' house is the only one on the street with the original stained glass windows, but it has the smallest garden

141. Xavier's house is near the cemetery

142. Deb's house is in a great location, but only has two bedrooms

143. Daniel's house is home to six cats and a bearded lizard

144. Judith's house has a kitchen with shocking pink walls

145. Ruth's house has a basement flat with a lodger, which helps with security

146. Doris' house has swings and fruit trees in the back garden

147. Lindsey's house is in a gated estate, and can be difficult to find

148. Joanne's house is a 1950s semi on the bus route to Stretford

149. Denise's house is "like a spaceship"

150. Alison's house had no furniture in the front room

151. Clare's house is decorated in a restful palette to offset the noise of the car park

152. Sara's house has a smell of wet dog, which reminds her of her childhood

153. Mark's house is in Northenden

154. Dee's house has two front paths

155. Ciara's house is surrounded by trees

156. Hugh's house is often used as a film location, which can be very lucrative

157. Geoff's house is a work in progress

158. Gwen's house is in Abergele

159. Meena's house is opposite an old church with a steeple, but the sound of ringing bells is faked

Two Hundred Houses

160. Flo's house is called "The Thorns"

161. Teddy's house has a loft conversion called "twin peaks", due to the double gabled windows

162. Ruth's house was open plan in the days before open plan

163. Adrian's house has a shared driveway

164. Jude's house was known as 'the big house"

165. Keith's house had a room for practising his posing routine

166. Lorraine's house had her hairdressing certificates framed and mounted on the walls

167. Ricky's house had a bath behind the kitchen

168. Elizabeth's house has window seats in the front bay

169. Katie's house is very neatly-kept

170. Jade's house has decorative pebbles in the fireplace

171. Jay's house had a chrome magazine rack and a breakfast bar

172. Brian's house is the Green Party's get-together venue

173. Joyce's house had the mingled smell of marijuana and flowers

174. Jasmine's house is near the mosque and parking is an issue

175. Violet's house is on a crescent

176. Mike's house was by the ship canal; boats would float past the end of his garden

177. Heather's house was a fixer-upper and sold for a lot of money

178. Rachel's house has a cellar with 1970s graffiti – "busted for smiling on a dull day"

179. Maz's house has a bathroom with gold-plated taps

Two Hundred Houses

180. Georges' house is now unrecognizable

181. Andrea's house has front gates which she fastens with a bike lock

182. Ali's house had a garden waist-deep in nettles

183. Sue's house is like a stately home

184. Janet's house is overlooking the park

185. Julie's house was on Laurel Avenue, and had a laurel in the front garden

186. Josh's house is near the Theatre of Dreams

187. Jean's house was on the Canadian border

188. Alex's house was all about women and cats

189. Gerry's house is round the corner from Josh's

190. Jennifer's house was the epitome of 1980s style, with a split-level cooker and a black kitchen

191. Jane's house had a garden with a view of the Peaks, which was perfect for summer picnics

192. Bernie's house had a dangerous staircase

193. Paula's house was right on a bend

194. Amanda's house is in the catchment area for very good schools

195. John's house had a statue of a rearing bull, called Toro

196. Jess's house has an Aga AND an electric oven in the kitchen

197. June's house was stuffed with breast pumps and teenagers

198. Jilly's house was enormous

199. Greg's house was very upmarket, which was a surprise

200. Rebecca's house is rented